You're Closer

Than You Think

5 Habits for Obtaining

Financial and Professional Success

by Teeba Rose

Teeba Rose

You're Closer Than You Think

Credits

Author	Teeba Rose
Co-Author / Editor	LaWanda Hill
Editor	Richard Zagrzecki
Editor	Terry Bessard
Media Consultant	Fred Burford III
Layout and Design	Fred Burford III
Photography	Dailey Hubbard

Teeba Rose

TABLE OF CONTENTS

FOREWORD

Acknowledgments

i

Teeba Rose

FOREWORD

Congratulations! If you are ready to learn and launch proven principles for taking your life to a more productive and prosperous level, you have come to the right book and a wise author.

You're Closer Than You Think was born from Teeba Rose's continuing unselfish desire to advise and encourage college students, professionals and entrepreneurs based on the results and rewards of his personal experience. When he realized over time he was repeating these key growth strategies (and when one of his mentees told him he should write a book), he made it his mission to put them in writing. You, dear reader, will be glad he did.

Within the pages of this book, Teeba, walks you through five major simple and powerful habits you can practice to maximize, manage, make, multiply and master key components for an enriched personal and professional life. The journey begins, as it always should, with you and how you choose (on and with purpose) to see and seize life.

From start to finish, Teeba reminds us all that we are free right now to be our own architects and that how we develop our blueprints has much to do with what we build – and enjoy. As you read this book, you will be encouraged, inspired and instructed by an author who is not afraid to share his hard-earned mistakes for your benefit and blessings. It is clear that he wants the best for you.

To that end, Teeba has developed a corresponding workbook with exercises that will help you take the five habits from words to action.

I encourage you to stop right now and thank the source that has brought you to *You're Closer Than You Think*, read (and re-read) it carefully, do as it and the workbook prescribes and go forth and prosper for you and your loved ones...and for generations to come.

- KIRBYJON H. CALDWELL

ACKNOWLEDGMENTS

"One man plants, another (wo)man waters, but only God can give the increase."

I have witnessed the manifestation of that truth from the start to completion of this book. To that end, there are many people who I would like to acknowledge and thank for carrying out their individual assignments in the process.

The original seeds of this project came from my father, Oscar Rose. Thank you, Dad, for repeatedly teaching me many of the concepts within this book. I did not get it the first time around, but I came to know how important the information was as I shared it with others. I am sure I learned many of your lessons much later than you had hoped for, but I appreciate and thank you greatly for your patience and love for me throughout the process.

Next, the idea of writing this book came from a good friend of mine, LaWanda Hill, who has been invaluable to me during this process. In 2009, when she moved to Houston to begin graduate school, she and I took on a mentor-mentee relationship. Much of the information I shared with her is found throughout this book. Thank you, LaWanda, for watering the belief that the world could benefit from the wisdom I have obtained and reminding me that everyone did not need to learn life's lessons the hard way.

Thank you to my Spanish teacher, Vasti Marcelo. As she was approaching her 27th birthday, she informed me she wanted a letter of wisdom from 27 individuals, and one of those individuals happened to be me. While sharing with her many of the principles discussed in this book, she shared how life-changing my words had been for her and her friendship circle. Thank you, Vasti, for watering the seed.

Next, I would like to thank my incredible wife, Courtney Johnson Rose. You have gone above and beyond in watering and attending to the many seeds of potential within me. For the last 11 years, you have been an inspiration to watch and share life with. You raise the bar constantly and then push it aside to create a higher one. You have not only consistently exercised each of the habits shared on the subsequent pages, but inspired me to do so as well. Thank you, Courtney, for being an amazing wife to me and outstanding mother. Thank you to my mother, Brenda Rose, for always being there for me and reminding me that all things are possible if you work smart and hard enough to achieve them.

Thank you to my stepmother, Lois Rose, and to my father-in-law and mother-in-law, George and Thomasine Johnson, for all of your love, support and encouragement. Being in the presence of each of you in some capacity gave me the inspiration I needed to keep moving forward in life and ultimately in my endeavor to write this book.

Thank you to my sister, Latonya Willrich, best friend, Fred Burford II, and to all of my family and friends for all of your support over the years. Thank you, Ashriel Dunham, for the many ways in which you helped me to refine my ideas and supported me throughout the journey. Thank you to Emmanuel Bernstein, who mentored me and taught me priceless business principles. Thanks, Lonnie Davis, for encouraging and inspiring me over the last 26 years as a mentor and friend.

Finally, I would like to thank God and acknowledge Him for being the one who gave increase to the original seed that was planted.

Teeba Rose

Chapter 1

MAXIMIZE YOUR TIME

People look at age as a mile marker, and to some degree it would be if you knew how long you would live. Since we do not know, I have discovered that learning to *Maximize Your Time* is a fundamental habit needed on the journey to success.

I believe we should all strive to maximize each moment we are granted. When someone has a life-altering moment, be it a death in the family, close call with fate or any other missed opportunity, the one thing you never hear them say is, "I am sure glad I do not have any more time." The beautiful thing for you, however, is that you do!

Maximize Your Freedom

Understanding the value of time is critical in pursuing success in general. Time well spent on your journey to success will make it all the more enjoyable. One beautiful thing about time is that it brings with it the **choice** to be free and enjoy life. It takes courage to be free in a world where people by habit will try their best to keep you boxed in.

Nevertheless, the choice is still ours.

With that beautiful gift, get in the habit of laughing as often as you can, even if no one else finds what you are laughing at comical. Make it a daily habit to love generously. Be yourself despite how others may judge you.

In the time that I have been blessed to traverse this planet, I have been amazed at how many people forego these choices each day at the expense of not enjoying life. Your time is not maximized if you are not enjoying life! If you identify as someone who is not operating as freely as you feel you ought to, today you can choose to live life differently. You can choose to laugh, give and receive love, and give yourself permission to be true to who you are.

What a shame it would be to look back over our book of life and discover that of the days we were granted, we spent 90 percent of them unengaged, angry, bitter and pretending to be someone we are not.

Maximize Each Day

In addition to maximizing your freedom, it is equally important to maximize each day. I believe the best way to accomplish this is to set short- and long-term goals.

When you get in the habit of setting goals, you will find you become more intentional about how you spend your time. Your energy and time will be driven by a goal. Establishing goals should be accompanied by a plan for achieving them. Your goal is the ultimate outcome, and your plans are the steps you take to achieve that outcome.

All successful people have set goals. Each have planned their work and worked their plan.

Your written plan serves as a point of reference. Depending on what you would like to accomplish, you may need to refer back to the plan daily, weekly, or even monthly. It does not have to be perfect. In fact, you should revise your plan consistently to make it better and more efficient.

You will use your plan to make the necessary adjustments that are inevitable on your journey to economic and professional success.

Each plan should have a daily action strategy, or what you might call a to-do list. Because your action plan will become your focus, you are more likely to complete your goals and less likely to become distracted when you have a plan of action.

Distractions are inevitable along your journey. However, establishing the habits outlined above will help you to manage these distractions and stay on track.

So in maximizing each day, you should always start with the big picture (short- and long-term goals), followed by an execution of the day-to-day, detail-oriented action plans/to-do lists.

At the end of each day, you want to ensure you have maximized your choice to be free and maximized each day. In doing so, you will find yourself one step closer to professional and financial success.

Reflection Moments:

Do you feel you have been maximizing your time? How much of your day is governed by the opinions of others?

Is it costing you your happiness?

List your short- and long-term goals.

List the plan required to achieve each goal.

You're Closer Than You Think

Chapter 2

MANAGE YOUR BRAND

Have you discovered you are always communicating to others both verbally and nonverbally? As a result, based on what you have communicated, many people have formed opinions about who you are.

I have found that although an individual may not show any indicator of it, he or she is always processing information you have communicated about yourself on some level and storing it away for later use. The information that he or she has processed about you will then be used to make very important professional decisions. Decisions that can impact your life for better or worse, open up doors of opportunity, and help you go from a local platform to a national one.

What you communicate about yourself to others is essentially your *brand*; the first thing that comes to mind for others when your name is mentioned. The qualities others attribute to you personally and professionally can be a good measure of how well you manage your brand.

Brand management is another important habit on your journey to financial and professional success. Brand management is something that we are always engaging in, whether intentionally or unintentionally. The beauty of managing your brand is that to a large extent, it can be within your control.

Professional Brand Management

Brand management is something all successful professionals have mastered.

Oprah Winfrey, Beyoncé, Bill Gates and Kevin Hart are all very different, but they share something in common: Each has been intentional about managing his or her brand.

Think about it. Each time their names are associated with anything, you know it will be of great quality. They have managed their brand by being consistent in their work ethic. They have been careful with their speech.

The causes they have aligned themselves with are an extension of some part of who they are or what they believe in. Even their attire is a reflection of the value they attribute to themselves. *You, too, can be a successful professional, consistent in your work ethic, careful with your speech and thoughtful about the people and things you choose to align yourself with.*

All these actions are a part of professional brand management. You see, you get to decide if others get to see your positive attributes. *The key to that is managing your professional brand by being intentional and consistent.*

Professional brand management is also about *intentionally refining and improving your brand so that it will increase in value, appeal and importance!* Your brand should always be something you are working to improve. As it improves, it should help open doors and assist you in getting the opportunities you desire to have.

The quality of your brand can generally be the reason someone wants to do business with you, or in some cases, why they may not. For instance, being the perfect fit for a job is about more than being the individual who has been at the company the longest or the person who is competent enough to carry out the duties of the job description. Being the perfect fit also entails whether your brand is one that fits easily in the position you want to have and is of high quality.

One important objective of the employer is to discern if your brand is an asset or liability. In other words, employers always will engage in quality control. They want to ensure that your professional brand is consistent with their own. Many people have found themselves passed over for an opportunity not because they had not worked for the employer long enough, but because their professional brand was inconsistent with the position they were seeking.

My wife is a real estate broker and an excellent example of managing your professional brand by employing the principles listed above. Since before she was born, her parents have owned a real estate firm. After completing high school, she knew the family business was something she desired to be a part of. She left for college to further her education so as to be *intentional about her brand development*.

Immediately after completing college, she obtained her real estate license to become a part-time real estate broker. She assisted a friend in purchasing a home. During that process, she was *consistent* in dependability, loyalty, professionalism, punctuality, respectfulness and positive optimism. She felt that these attributes were a *reflection of her core values* and intentionally wanted them to be associated with her professional brand.

She considered each experience with a new client as an opportunity to **improve in the quality of service she provided**. Over time, these positive attributes are what she became known for. As a result, she increased in *appeal* when compared to other real estate brokers. Within two years, she had built a part-time referral business that generated as much income as her full-time job.

She knew early on about professional brand management. She endeavored to protect and nourish her brand so that it could serve her well in the future. You, too, can do the same if you start this habit now.

Hopefully you, like my wife and other professionals, have been working to perfect your professional brand by being intentional in your pursuits to ensure that your actions are a clear reflection of your core values. If you have not done so, you can start today!

Personal Brand Management

Your successful professional brand can only be as

great as your personal brand. Your personal brand is essentially an extension of yourself. How well you manage yourself is critical to overall brand management.

Consider as an example that your personal brand is an invisible business card you carry with you and distribute to others you meet. Then ask yourself what pile would your business card be placed in by the majority of those people? What types of conclusions would they draw about your personal brand based on your interactions together?

Would they classify you in the "always has an excuse" pile? Would you be in the "very considerate" pile? What about "always has to have the last word" or "only listens to speak, never to understand"? The answers to those questions are essential as they will impact the perception of your overall brand.

In addition to what others have to say about your personal brand, what insight do you have about yourself? Have you identified the environments in which you thrive? How well you handle pressure and manage frustration? How adaptable you are to change? These are all very important questions that reflect your strengths and weaknesses as a person and inevitably what others think about your personal brand.

I am amazed at when people say, "I do and dress for my approval only, and do not care what other people say or think about it." While that may be true, you may not want the results of what this type of thinking can do to the perception of your personal brand. The perception of others will determine if and how they wish to proceed with you.

Just as important as the way you manage yourself is the way in which you manage your personal associations.

Associations matter. People tend to associate with others who are more like themselves in many ways. We tend to associate with individuals we aspire to be like in some capacity.

I personally believe we are the average of the five people we associate with the most, so think critically when choosing the five people you spend the most time with. Ultimately, it will impact your personal brand, either positively or negatively. Some individuals are only interested in associating with people who are just as driven, ambitious and goal-oriented as they are. While other individuals may feel more comfortable associating with people who are content with what life may bring them.

Through this five-people method, there is great benefit. For instance, you may find new strategies and solutions to problems you simply cannot solve on your own. Your top five could be individuals who propel you along your journey, or they may play a part in your stagnation.

I am in no way suggesting you disassociate from your current friends or become overly critical of others. However, I am suggesting you begin to think critically about the individuals you spend the most time with and assess if they are helping or hindering you in your pursuit of improved brand management.

This may not happen overnight. You may not even need to stop associating completely with anyone in particular in your top five. But, you just might need to limit your association with some while increasing your association with others.

Start pondering the quality of your professional brand and the perception others have of your personal brand. What picture of you would come to mind if I were to mention your name to people who know you?

When I take my photo for my driver's license every few years, I make sure to smile, which is a better representation of who I am. I realized early on that I would be giving my license to a lot of people over the course of my lifetime.

If you use that philosophy when thinking about the persona you choose to display to people, both personally and professionally, hopefully it will decrease the number of instances in which you feel your brand has been misrepresented.

Think about the times you have heard people say, "Do not look at the photo on my license because it is not a good picture of me." What would happen if we were more conscious of the fact that we are presenting a picture of ourselves personally and professionally with each personal and public encounter? Would it decrease the instances in which we would have to say, "That is not a good picture of me?" If you choose to make managing your brand a habit, it can be.

Reflection Moments:

What are your core values?

Can others easily recognize your core values in your professional work ethic?

What personal attributes do you find most important that you would like to leave with others?

How can you begin to manage your brand today?

List the five people you associate with the most and identify their personal and professional attributes that have helped to improve your brand.

Chapter 3

MAKE EXTRAORDINARY A HABIT

Many people are willing to put in an average amount of effort to achieve an average outcome. However, very few people are willing to put in an extraordinary amount of effort in order to obtain an extraordinary outcome.

The mistake most people make is not found in the outcome they desire in life. The mistake is not realizing the pathway to that place starts with an extraordinary work ethic. If you are to arrive at your desired destination of professional and financial success, you will have to learn to make extraordinary a habit, despite where you currently are in your journey of success.

Extraordinary Work Ethic

Extraordinary work ethic is the bridge that connects where you are to where you are trying to go. Simply put, you cannot get to the next level without it. Work ethic should be motivated by intrinsic values and your desired level of success. That is, the quality and effort you put into your work must come from within.

Having an extraordinary work ethic means you have resolved to give your best at all times. You see giving your best is about you and no one else. You owe it to yourself and to the gifts and talents you have on the inside of you to be the best you.

Sure, outside factors can impact your motivation, but you will have to learn to be self-motivated despite those forces, even if it means you are in an environment you find to be only ordinary.

I have learned that most people do not practice this habit. They allow their circumstances and external factors to determine the effort they put forth. Where they are determines what they give. That mindset is far from helpful. Many have allowed an ordinary work environment to deflate their motivation to be extraordinary. But I say, "Be the person that shifts ordinary work environments to extraordinary."

Whatever work environment you find yourself in, you must make the decision today to learn something in everything you do and look for ways to make improvements.

Try your best not to be concerned with whether

you receive immediate credit for what you do. Do not restrict your growth by being anything less than extraordinary just because your work ethic may not instantly pay off.

Gratification is not always immediate. In fact, it is delayed in most cases. But the price you pay is so small when compared to what you eventually will receive. Your desired level of success should be worth the work ethic it will take to achieve it.

So many people have failed to move forward in life because they have allowed external influences such as pay grade, supervisors, ordinary organizations or an inability to accept delayed gratification to rob them of the opportunity to make extraordinary a work habit.

Do not allow yourself to fall victim to this mistake! Do not succumb to a draining process of monotony. Give it all you have!

Extraordinary Outcomes

I often say that you need to have the mindset of an entrepreneur, not an employee. With an employee mindset, you are inclined to fall victim to doing just enough to get by. Subsequently, your employer may then decide to pay you just enough not to quit.

Doing your best is just as much for you as it is for your employer. The idea that doing only what is required is the same thinking that puts you in a box of mediocrity. When you have an entrepreneur mindset, you want to ensure that the task is accomplished, not just that effort was put into it regardless of the outcome. You do not have to own your own business to think about the impact your part ultimately plays in whatever you are doing.

Always ask yourself this: If you owned the company yet decided to work in your current position, what would you do differently? Would you follow through more? Would you ensure that certain tasks were accomplished to the best of your ability?

Better yet, if you knew that your bonus was attached to your success, would you do anything differently? While you may not own the company, you do own your work ethic and your brand. By making extraordinary a habit, you will feel better about your work and always be ready for future opportunities when they come along.

The entrepreneur's mentality is that excuses are not an option, and the extra mile is required because it is your success on the line. Entrepreneurs understand it is the work ethic they develop at their current level that ultimately will lead them to the next level of success. Fight the urge to be mediocre.

My mother-in-law always quotes the Bible by saying, "All labor is profit." What she means by this is that your hard work never goes in vain. Even if you do not see the reward today of going the extra mile, learning a new skill, helping someone or simply doing your best no matter the cost, I assure you that someday it will pay off.

The skills you obtain from completing a project or finishing a task ahead of schedule may not seem to matter, and often may seem to have been a waste of time and labor. But one day, you will need the skills you have just learned, the relationship you have just cultivated and the confidence to know what you are capable of and you will have it.

Ordinary people tend to get ready to handle the new opportunity. Extraordinary people stay ready because they know that an opportunity is coming. So while someone may say, "I have done all of this for nothing," an extraordinary habit would be to know that all labor is profit and while you may not use it today, what you have done will pay off tomorrow.

I remember one of my first jobs growing up was waiting tables at a large Mexican restaurant in Houston. When I started working there, I was so bad that I almost did not make it through the initial training. I was having a hard time memorizing all of the menu items and understanding the computer system. I would ride the bus to training, which was at another location because the restaurant was still under construction and had not yet opened.

I remember thinking, "If I can just make it through training, I will make an excellent waiter." Well, I finally completed the training, and the restaurant opened shortly thereafter.

Everyone was new, and they all looked out for themselves. There was very little camaraderie or team spirit. The overall thinking among the waitstaff was to just serve their assigned customers and not do much else.

We have all been to a restaurant where you need something and no one will even give you eye contact, let alone lend a hand without you stopping them and asking for it. Think about it. How much more time does it really take for a person to look around to see if anyone needs something before they leave the table next to yours?

My mentality was simple: If I helped my customers and then spent a little extra time helping yours, we would all make better tips and have a great working environment, and the customers would come back, which would boost everyone's income.

Customers soon began asking for me by name, and I was promoted to trainer. I continued to make extraordinary a habit, and I treated this restaurant just like I would my own business.

The managers saw my work ethic, and I was further promoted to bartender then manager. I worked my way up to being third in charge at this well-known restaurant. One of the key perks this led to was when my sister got married, the general manager allowed me to use his discount to pay for the food for her wedding. It cost my sister $2.50 per person to feed all of her guests.

Why is this story important? Because it all started with making extraordinary a habit.

While working at that restaurant, I met Lonnie Davis, who later became my mentor. He did not live in Houston, but whenever he was in town visiting his friend Elizabeth, they would eat at the restaurant and ask for me by name.

During one of those visits, Lonnie told me I would be great in marketing. I had never thought about it before. He said that when I graduated, give him a call, and he would see what he could do to get me hired at one of the largest copier companies in the world.

As a result, after graduation I had a job making $20,000 more than I would have had I not met Lonnie and Elizabeth. You see, they had witnessed me making extraordinary a habit and were willing to tell others on my behalf. All Labor Is Profit.

Making extraordinary a habit will indeed help you to reach your goals. You will be a motivation and inspiration to many people, young and old. The question that you will be asked most often is, "How did you get started?" When you think back to this moment, you will remember it was the day you figured out you were not operating at 100 percent. You can tell them that it was the day that you decided to make extraordinary a habit.

Reflection Moments:

Are you operating at your full potential right now?

In what areas are you not?

What areas of your life would you like to see extraordinary results?

How can you start increasing your input in order to see your desired outputs?

You're Closer Than You Think

Chapter 4

MULTIPLY YOUR INCOME

I love agriculture because I believe many of the principles associated with it are applicable to life. Think about it. A seed represents both what you have now and what you desire to have in the future.

For the sake of this chapter, let us think of your seed as finances. The process of planting and growing financial seeds, much like agricultural seeds for a farmer, necessitates time, discipline and patience.

The abundant harvest that results from those critical elements speaks to the fundamental principle that something that originally is small can blossom into something much greater with time and consistency.

What I have discovered over time is that while many enjoy a harvest of tasty and healthy fruit, or in your case a harvest of healthy finances, few are willing to employ what it takes to achieve it. Today is the day that you employ what is shared in this chapter in order to achieve abundant and healthy finances. Today is the day you commit to multiplying your income!

I should warn you, however, that to multiply your income, it will take an adjusted mindset. Like the habits we have discussed so far, the earlier you start, the better!

Adjust Your Mindset

My father would tell me, "Don't blow all of your money" and "Do you really need that?"

But I often heard from so many others, "If you want something, save your money and buy it." As a child and, unfortunately, many times as an adult, that is exactly what I did. I internalized the idea that money is to be saved and then to be spent. Although I started the habit early on of saving to buy, it was at the expense of saving to invest.

Each time I spent all of my money on something that I wanted, I was at the same time putting myself in a perpetual state of starting over with nothing. It is the result of a "spending mindset" versus an "investing mindset." While we have earned every right to spend our hard-earned money on what we desire, I believe we sometimes forget that spending as much as we receive is not profitable.

In order to profit from what you earn, you must

learn the critical components necessary to multiply your income. That means you must learn to become better at saving AND investing. This mindset adjustment can benefit you for the rest of your life.

Adjusting Your Financial Distribution

After you have adjusted your mindset, the next step is to adjust your financial distribution. I mentioned earlier that there are two mindsets: spender and investor.

Part of having an investor's mindset is to be intentional and disciplined about your financial distributions. This is something that varies significantly among people. In order to keep it simple, I will share the four distributions that are essential to me, and you can make adjustments to the sample I provide.

The four distributions that are critical in my example are giving, saving, investing and living.

I am a firm believer that giving of your time, talents, and treasures will benefit you and others. Giving not only makes the world a better place, it simultaneously brings a joy that nothing else can provide. If you have not experienced the joy I speak about, try giving your time, talents and treasures to others.

In addition to giving, saving is very important. If you do not have the discipline to save, then you will not get to a place where you can multiply your income.

Next is investing. That is the point of this entire chapter! Investing will make your income profitable in the long run.

Finally, living is how we survive, so unquestionably it is a part of my financial distribution. In order to live, I believe you must set a budget and a plan for sticking with it. Without a budget, you may find it difficult, if not impossible, to live within a certain portion of your income. Your budget also will be able to show you when you are ahead and when you may need to cut back to accomplish your goals.

I strongly believe these four distributions are not an exhaustive list but definitely a critical starting point in multiplying your income. You can apply your financial distribution intentionally, no matter how much money you earn or how old you are. Take a look below at the percentages allocated to my financial distributions.

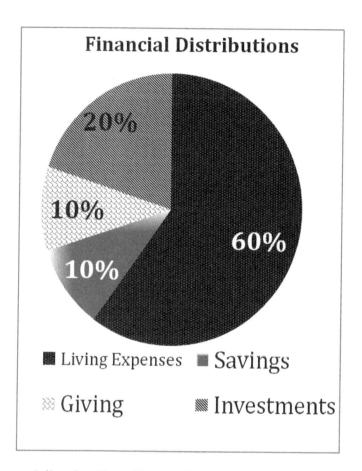

Financial Distributions

- Living Expenses
- Savings
- Giving
- Investments

Adjusting Your Financial Habits

Now imagine for a moment that you employed this financial distribution chart from age five to 85. As a five-year-old, you were given an allowance by your parents and decided you wanted to use it to purchase a new toy that you wanted. What if your parents told you that in addition to saving money for your toy, you also should consider how you will make a profit from your allowance?

But what on earth can a five-year-old invest in? The answer is simple. Perhaps a lemonade stand, rare comic books or coins. There are a number of things.

At the end of a few months, not only have you purchased the toy you wanted, but you have begun the process of conditioning your mindset to save and invest. As a child, you can get what you desire and position yourself early on to learn how to have money that is ready to go to work for you.

As time passes and you grow into adulthood, this habit would become second nature to you. Each time you have money coming in, you would distribute a portion to living, giving, saving and investing. Over time, you will have accomplished a great deal. You will have made the world a better place by giving, obtained what you desired by saving and experienced an abundance of healthy finances by investing. But in order to get to this place of abundant finances, discipline and restraint are critical.

Although I have obtained financial success, had I

been disciplined enough to practice and maintain this habit, I would be much further along.

I would like for you to not make the same mistakes that I did. Instead, you can learn from mine and save yourself the time and difficulty that I experienced. For example, when I was 17, my father recommended I purchase a piece of rental property. His idea was I would continue to live at home with him, and the rental property would be my entry into the process of accumulating financial wealth.

My father's cousins owned several rental properties and, naturally, they and my father shared with me the importance of investing in real estate. My father even suggested he and I could fix any problems that would come up because he is extremely handy.

He knew how critical it is to distribute a portion of your income to investing, and I had not quite shifted my mindset to adopt that philosophy.

He knew that in a few years not only would the property be paid in full, but I would be able to leverage my financial abilities and borrow against it if I ever needed anything.

Unfortunately, I had a spender's mindset while my father had an investor's mindset. I had a healthy fear of investing because I had never done it before nor had I disciplined myself to set aside a portion of my income for this purpose.

Despite my father's efforts, I did not show interest in learning this process due to my lack of discipline and financial immaturity. The investing part of my financial distribution chart was non-existent. This resulted in a missed opportunity to sow financial seeds and receive an abundant harvest. Rather than using the money I had saved to purchase a rental property, I foolishly used it to purchase a $25,000 new car, which resulted in a $450 monthly car note.

Reflecting on this missed opportunity years later with my dad, he told me the rental property he wanted me to purchase would have cost $30,000. My heart sank at that moment because I realized my financial immaturity had caused me to miss a turning point in my economic future. Rather than purchase a car for $25,000 and pay $450 a month, I could have bought the rental property for $30,000 with a mortgage of $400 a month. Subsequently, I could have rented the property to someone for $1,000 per month. This would have resulted in a $400 profit for me each month after expenses.

After nearly 6 ½ years of applying the monthly profits of $400 per month ($400 x 75mo. = $30,000, plus the standard monthly payments to the mortgage) I would have owned my first asset. I would have been in position to make a profit of $800 every month / $9,600 a year and with no additional daily work involved.

I could have then used this profit to purchase my second investment property, then my third and fourth. Each time I would have paid off a property, it would have allowed me to buy the next one faster because I would have used the profits from the previous ones. But you see, this financial harvest would have required the proper mindset. It also required time, patience and discipline the process of planting and reaping an abundant harvest requires — all of which I did not have at the time.

In order to see the implications of this poor decision, consider the financial position I would have been in when going to purchase my second property 6 1/2 years later. I would have been able to take the monthly profit of $400 per month plus the $800 I was earning from the first property and pay off the second property in just two years.

By this time, I would be have been around 25 years old with $1,600 ($800 x two properties) per month worth of disposable income. When I would have purchased my third property for $45,000 using the $800 profit per month from my first property, the $800 per month profit from my second property and the $500 a month profit from the third property (because I have a tenant paying $1,200 per month on a home with a mortgage payment of $500 = $500 profit after expenses), it would have only taken me roughly two years to pay off my third property. I would have been putting $2,100 per month into the third property.

I would have done it again on my fourth property, which means I would have been 30 years old with $3,600 per month or $43,200 per year coming in before I would have stepped foot into my job. Today, those same properties are selling for $90,000. That was 25 years ago. I would have earned over a million dollars to date and have $400,000 worth of assets based off that one decision to purchase an investment over the purchase of a new car.

Not only would I be a millionaire today, but that one good decision would have encouraged other smarter and wiser financial decisions. Although that figure is only an estimate and does not take into account the cost of taxes, repairs and insurance, it is relatively close to the profit that I could have obtained.

Another missed opportunity for a harvest of financial abundance occurred when I was 25. The brother of a friend of mine brought an idea to me regarding a new restaurant he was planning to open in Houston. I had managed a successful restaurant throughout college, and my friend's brother was looking for investors and good employees.

He shared the company's business plan with me and the amount of money he was looking to raise and gave me an opportunity to invest. We went to the site of where the restaurant would be located and he shared with me how this small location would be able to serve thousands of clients. He adequately addressed each of my reservations.

This time, instead of not being willing to invest, I had not distributed my finances appropriately, so I did not have the money available to invest. You might say that I was all show and no true wealth.

Yes, I made great money and lived well at the

time, which is one of the reasons we were even having this conversation, but I had not been preparing myself for this day. So I did what anyone else would have done, and I went back to my father and shared the business plan with him, explaining everything that had been told to me.

My father gave me the statistics of the number of restaurants that fail each year and said he was not willing to invest the money in a restaurant on my behalf. You see, my father tried to put me in the right position of strength so that I could have been able to make that decision on my own when the time came, but I did not listen. As a result, I was not ready when this opportunity presented itself and I had to decline the investment offer.

Today, it is a thriving restaurant with lines of customers wrapped around the building waiting to get in and enjoy the food and atmosphere.

When visitors from across the country come to the city and ask where they should go for great food, they are directed straight to this restaurant. It has become just what the gentleman said it would be: a must-dine experience.

Those who did invest in it are still receiving

dividends from that one-time investment. This reminds me that opportunities do not disappear, they just go away from you and end up with others who are prepared to receive them.

Adjust Your Financial Outcomes

Let my failures and poor decisions be enough for the both of us today! Adjust your mindset, financial distributions and financial habits. If you can do this, you will inevitably adjust your financial outcomes.

If you can commit to the time, discipline and patience it takes, money will never be an issue for you again. You will be able to travel, shop and invest in the things you enjoy, while being able to retire earlier from your job.

You will no longer need to do things as a result of how much money you make because money would begin to work for you. You will have learned to multiply your income. The world would be at your fingertips waiting on your request. You could become a venture capitalist investing in companies, stocks or small businesses. You do not need to start grand; you can start from right where you are today.

If you are living at home or with your family, continue to do so and employ the habits I outlined in this chapter. What difference does it make that you have your own place but are just doing "OK" and living off 100 percent of your income. I would like to encourage you not to rush out to live on your own. Rather, rush to be in a position of power and leverage.

If you have only one stream of income, consider adding others. After all, the more financial seeds you plant, the greater the harvest you can expect. For some individuals, one stream of income will only cover living expenses. That is OK. There is still room to grow and multiply your income. You can begin by brainstorming ideas for additional streams of income. They can be anything you desire them to be.

Streams of Income Examples

1.   Job
2.   Rental Property
3.   Stocks/ Financial Planner
4.   New Business
5.   Extra Job
6.   Assets that appreciate in value

As you begin brainstorming about additional streams of income, think about businesses and ideas that will pay well until you can do what you desire to do. Remember, the small sacrificial seeds you sow today will result in an abundant harvest in the future.

I had this same conversation with a friend of mine who is a Spanish teacher by profession. As we discussed additional streams of income, she did not know where to begin. I informed her that by using her professional skill set, she could teach students Spanish privately and earn additional income.

She then began to wonder about what most people worry about first — where would she get her clients? I replied that my son would be her first student because we wanted him to learn Spanish. Later that day, my wife and I took our son to a birthday party, where we saw one of my wife's friends. As we began to chat, I told her about the possibility of our son taking Spanish classes on the weekend. She said she wanted her two daughters to also take the classes.

I called my friend and let her know that she was already up to three clients, and that there were plenty of other parents I knew who wanted their children to learn a second language as well. If she taught a small group of 10 students for two hours on Saturdays and charged $15 per hour, she could make $300 per Saturday and $1,200 per month. This is an additional $14,400 revenue in just one year.

I helped her find a location to teach the students that would cost her $20 an hour to use, which adds up to $960 per year. She has friends who work in marketing who can create any printed material she needs. To print fliers would cost her roughly $250. After paying taxes on the remaining $13,190 (which is about 15 percent), she would be left with an additional $11,211 for the year. That is not bad for an additional stream of income using two hours on a Saturday to help meet a financial goal. Now that she has found a way to begin to get on track, she will need the time, discipline and patience to stay on track.

This is just an example of what she could do. What is your talent? What do you currently do at work that you could do part-time to earn additional income? My hope is that your creative wheels are starting to turn. While it was not mentioned in the section above, when creating a business, please note that you should also create an LLC, obtain any needed licenses, and budget for taxes you may have to pay.

Now is the time for you to work on your first investment, adjust your mindset, reconsider your financial distributions and increase your streams of income. In 10 to 13 years, you could be much further ahead by using the financial seeds you have in your pockets today. So what are you waiting for? Get started now, no matter how big or small the venture! Cancel the thought that you have to have it all together to start. Remember, the small seeds sown today are what lead to the abundant harvest of tomorrow. I trust that you will start sowing today.

Reflection Moments:

Have you seen the financial harvest that you desire?

List the categories in which your finances are currently distributed.

How can you adjust your distributions to reflect the recommended guidelines listed in this chapter?

List at least two additional streams of income you are willing to pursue.

You're Closer Than You Think

Chapter 5

MASTER THE FUNDAMENTALS AND SKILLS OF MANAGING CREDIT

When should I start building my credit? What constitutes good credit and how do I get it? How do I maintain a good credit standing? These are three questions that I am asked often by many people from many diverse walks of life. Before any of these questions can be answered, I believe it is critical to understand the fundamental rules associated with credit in general.

When engaging in any activity in which success is a potential outcome, there are always rules of engagement. How skilled you are at managing the rules is largely correlated with the level of success you will obtain. If you are not aware or understand the fundamental rules, inevitably you will lose to others who are more knowledgeable.

In addition to the rules of engagement, there are always critical elements that require skills to manage. The more advanced you are in managing these elements, the greater likelihood you are of obtaining success. To that end, in order to answer the three questions, I believe you must have a good working knowledge of the rules of engagement and acquire the skills necessary to manage the critical component of financial credit.

Acquiring the Fundamentals

Essentially, credit is the ability to obtain goods or services before paying. Moreover, a credit score is comparable to a risk assessment.

That risk assessment is determined by several factors, including your **payment history** (what has happened), **credit mix** (who you have engaged in a financial relationship with), **new credit** (with whom have you started a new relationship) and **length of credit history** (how long you have been engaging in credit-worthy activity in those relationships).

A number of things relating to these factors are reported, including payment activity and whether financial debt was paid off early, late or never. Each line of credit you have is also reported, including credit cards, car notes, mortgages, rental history, department store accounts, and lines of credit with banks, as well as any other debtor that you may owe.

Each of these components are reported to credit

bureaus on a monthly basis. Based on the skill you demonstrate in managing these factors, you will be labeled either a low credit risk or a high credit risk. A low credit risk will be reflected in a higher credit score. A high credit risk will be reflected in a low credit score.

There are three main credit bureaus: Equifax, Trans Union and Experian. Each reports differently, but based on what you are attempting to acquire, the general rule of thumb is that companies take the average or middle score of the three to determine your credit score.

Acquiring the Skill

Acquiring the fundamental rules of engagement is only half the battle in obtaining the financial credit outcome you desire. The remaining half is acquiring and further developing the skills necessary to manage the critical factors of financial credit. Remember, the more advanced you become in these skills, the more likely you are to achieve your desired financial credit outcome.

One of the first critical skills is to be frugal. When you are frugal, you are cautious and critical about the money you spend. In living this way, you will find there are a number of different ways to save money. Please start establishing and living by those ways.

I will give you a head start by sharing a very important piece of knowledge that you can add to your list. Immediately following the holidays, everything usually goes on sale. This means that in many instances, you will be able to afford 10 times as much of the pre-sale items.

Here is the perfect opportunity to save money and purchase gifts that are considered "off season" for the next year. Because they are not "in season," everyone has stopped making purchases for those items. Everyone except you!

This is the time you should be purchasing birthday presents and other items. If you buy next year's summer clothes just before winter, you will be getting them at 80 percent off. The same applies to Christmas and other holidays.

It is wise to store things for when the time comes but it is not wise to pay 85 percent for an item because a retailer marked it down by 15 percent. In the previous chapter, I shared that you should strive to live off of 60 percent of your income. This is one of the ways to ensure that your 60 percent goes further and you obtain the things you desire.

There is also a way to be frugal so that you can start working toward the financial credit outcome you desire. In addition to shopping in the off season, you can purchase most of the items you want online because in many instances, it will be much cheaper.

I realize that online shopping may not be your preference for some items, but for others it definitely should be. I also realize that these are not the most popular ways to shop, and it will involve planning. It definitely will require discipline to manage your spending impulses and time to get adjusted to the change. However, ultimately it will save you money, and that is a skill necessary in the overall management of your credit.

Another critical skill that I would like to discuss is minimizing what you purchase on credit. Credit is not designed to live off. On the surface, purchasing items on credit and paying for them for months and years seems like it is not that big of a deal. But ask yourself the question, "If I am paying for something on sale with a credit card and paying interest on something that I bought over a month ago, am I really getting a good deal?" By the time you have finished paying the additional interest on the sales item, was it really cheaper?

In most cases, the answer to those questions are no. You will have paid even more than the original price once you factor in the interest to purchase that item on credit. Challenge yourself to not allow your long-term options to change based on short-term decisions.

Let us consider this example for further clarity. Assume you have a friend named Hill. Hill is willing to loan you $5,000 to purchase an item you really desire. Hill, however, asks that in return, you pay 15 percent interest for the $5,000 she lends you until all of the money is paid back. On the surface, that sounds like a good idea, right?

Now consider that when the time comes for you to pay back Hill, you do not quite have all of the money, and you want to know if you can reimburse her over a period of time. Hill agrees to grant you this request, as she understands that life can at times be unpredictable.

However, now it has taken you two years of very

small payments to pay back Hill all you owed her. After looking back at the experience, you realized that the item you purchased became broken and outdated, yet you were still paying Hill for it.

Additionally, you realized you ended up paying Hill $2,000 of interest for something that not only is broken and outdated, but wasn't even a necessity.

The most significant point of this story is that credit is not designed for you to live off. It is designed to assist you in acquiring things temporarily. If you are going to pay interest for something that you are buying on sale, you have to ask yourself is it really a good deal.

Just like the earlier example when you borrowed the money from your friend Hill, in some cases you will have paid more for the item than the original price once you add the interest that the credit card company has charged you. Would it not be a better use of your money to purchase that item when it is 80 percent cheaper? I hope you now can find an appreciation for this skill.

A second critical skill is practicing patience and restraint. When you open up lines of credit, aim for minimal utilization of the credit line. That is, aim to use no more than 10 percent to 30 percent of the available credit. You may be asking yourself, "Why would I use only a small portion of the credit line?"

The answer is because you are trying to build your credit. Additionally, you are not trying to be in debt and pay high amounts of interests.

Think of your credit score as you would a report card in school. The student with an "A" in multiple subjects gets rewarded with 15 additional minutes for recess while everyone else may have to stay inside to do extra studying. Those students require extra studying because their grades reflect they have not grasped an exceptional understanding of each subject.

Likewise, by utilizing only 10 percent to 30 percent of your credit limit, you are proving you can and have become exceptional in the different domains of financial credit. You have proven you can manage your money, employ patience and utilize restraint. Therefore, you are given additional rewards while others must pay extra to get what you have.

You are proving that much like the student in the example used above, you have a good understanding of the subject matter. Consequently, you will be rewarded appropriately. Everyone, and by everyone I mean those granting credit lines, wants to know they are extending credit to someone who can practice patience and restraint. Once you have proven to have patience and restraint over a small amount, you will then be granted greater amounts.

After speaking with a loan officer, I learned that the best credit card scenario is for you to have a $300 limit and have a balance of $10 to $30. Once the bill arrives, you can pay it off, but the following day you can use it to buy lunch and keep the balance for the remainder of the month, repeating the process.

Please notice I am not suggesting you live off credit nor utilize more than 10 percent to 30 percent of the credit limit. These two skills of financial credit management will help you build your credit. Over time, your credit score will increase significantly, and you will have more buying power and a lower interest rate.

This graph below depicts the factors in which your credit risk (credit score) is determined. It includes the factors we discussed earlier in the chapter: your payment history, current debt, length of credit history, credit mix and new credit.

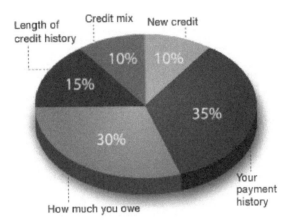

Matt Schulz (2011). Fie Pie Chart (chart). Retrieved from http://www.creditcards.com/credit-card-news/how-your-fico-credit-score-is-calculated-1270.php

Given the weight that how much money you owe to current debtors plays in determining your credit score, you can see that paying off debt while leaving other debts high will cause your credit to suffer.

A goal to strive for is a financial credit picture in which you utilize no more than 10 percent to 30 percent of the available credit limit and you have several areas of credit. However, you must be cautious, as too many lines of credit can hurt you as well. The two most important variables depicted in the pie graph are consistent timely payments and not maxing out your debt limit with any creditor.

Acquiring Your Desired Credit Score

Over your lifetime, your credit rating can mean the difference between paying the minimum or paying four to eight times more than you need to. So trust that the skills discussed above are ones you should strive to master.

Many times, we look at individuals who make the same amount of money as we do and see they have acquired much more than us. I believe that this is a result of knowledge of the fundamentals of financial credit as well as an employment of the skills discussed above.

For example, let us compare an individual who has obtained an "A" and has a 750 credit score and an individual who has obtained a "B" with a 520 credit score. For the sake of this example, both of these individuals earn $40,000 per year.

	Person A	**Person B**
Credit score	750	520
Living In	1,500sq.ft. house	1,000sq.ft.apartment
Cost per mo.	$1,600 per month	$1,900 per month
	Buying	Renting
Car$ per mo.	2013 Honda $350	2010 Honda $450
Car Insurance	$80 per month	$100 per month
Credit Cards	9% interest	22% interest
Jobs	No restrictions	Credit restrictions

This example depicts two similar individuals with significantly different realities. Both earn the same amount of money each year and appear to have similar living expenses. However, Individual "A" lives in a house, is working toward owning a home, pays lower interest rates, and pays less for a newer model car and auto insurance. Meanwhile Individual "B" has a very different reality. This individual lives in a smaller apartment, is not working toward ownership, pays higher interest rates for credit purchases, and pays more for an older model car and auto insurance . In this example, individual "A" has an additional $420 per month to put toward saving, investing and giving.

Once individual "A" begins to follow these habits, the gap between their incomes and lifestyles will begin to widen even more.

Putting It All Together

The reality is you do not need a lot of credit to build or improve your credit score. If you do have a line or lines of credit and desire to improve them, apply what you gleaned from the last chapter to rework the way you are distributing your finances.

You also want to work toward only 10 percent to 30 percent utilization of each of your credit lines. Next, be sure to make more than the minimum payments. Your goal is to pay down your debt as quickly as possible so that you are not paying a ridiculous amount in interest. By doing so, you are showing creditors that although your history may not be grand, you are working toward a better future.

Over time, you are showing those who will make the decision about extending a credit line to you that you have consistently paid on time for an extended period (time) with only 10 percent to 30 percent credit utilization (activity). Remember that these are two of the five critical factors involved in determining your credit risk.

If you do not have a major credit card (Visa / MasterCard), apply for two of them. If you cannot get a line of credit, you can always get a secured line of credit. An example of a secured line of credit is you going to the bank and giving them $1,000 for which you then ask for a loan for $1,000. You would then make monthly payments on the $1,000 you just borrowed. This is important because you are proving your ability to pay a line of credit (loan) from the bank on time.

Resist the temptation to open a line of credit by purchasing something grand, such as a car or something from a department store. If you purchase a car, you will be able to show that you can make timely payments (history), but you will have a long way to go before you can free up that amount of money (debt) that the car cost, which will increase your debt-to-income ratio (activity). If you owe too much debt, this communicates to those who wish to extend credit to you that while you make money, you spend almost as much as you make. That will impact your credit score and likely make you a high credit risk.

Now let us consider purchasing an expensive item from a department store. Assume for a moment that you open a department store line of credit in order to buy a $2,000 television. In that one transaction, you would have immediately maxed out the line of credit. Rather than utilizing only 10 percent to 30 percent of the credit line, you would have utilized 100 percent. By doing this, you would not be harming — not improving — your credit.

My hope is that this chapter, along with the examples provided, will give you a better understanding and appreciation of financial credit. Further, it is my hope that you will be inspired to start employing the skills necessary to better manage your financial credit.

After applying the fundamentals and the skills listed throughout this chapter, you will have made it clear to those extending credit lines that you are a low credit risk. The great part about that decision is there is always room for improvement. So, if you are a high risk right now, you do not always have to be. And if you are a low risk, there is still room for greater benefits and rewards for maintaining your low-risk status.

Reflection Moments:

List the rules of engagement and critical habits necessary for managing financial credit.

Which of the habits listed can you improve?

How will you start?

What are your financial credit goals for the next six months?

Chapter 6

FINAL THOUGHTS

Your individual journey to financial and professional success doesn't have to be a difficult one. There is a cost for success, and you have to mentally decide if you are willing to pay it. The price consists of sacrifice, time, patience, discipline, fortitude and energy.

There will be times throughout your journey when you will be challenged and wish the steps to the next level were easier. Do not wish it were easier; continue to work to become better and it will become easier for you. If accomplishing the goals that you have set for yourself were easy, then everyone already would have achieved them.

There will be times when you feel like giving up. Just remember that winners have found more ways that do not work than anyone else. They are rewarded for continuously coming back to find the one way that does work.

But all winners have one thing in common, and that is a lot of failures and refusing to quit. Do not be afraid to get knocked down or to fail. You have only truly failed if you let your last unsuccessful attempt be your last.

I encourage you to push through these challenges while also remaining patient with your journey. For every obstacle you will face, there is a solution. The reason you will be rewarded with your outcome is because you are willing to continue to search for that solution. Be willing to try new ways to achieve your goals. No one ever applauds you for what you would do or for potential. The world only rewards you for the goals you actually accomplish.

It was once said that in life, you are rewarded based on the size of the problems that you can solve. If you can only solve small problems, then you will only have a small reward. But those who can solve the more-complex problems are always rewarded for doing so. Remember, you do not have to know everything about everything to reach your goals, but you do have to seek the answers and apply them to move forward and attain your desired success. As I stated at the start of this book, it is OK to take a break. But it is not OK to quit and walk away forever.

In addition to the price you will pay in effort, I

must also caution you to be prepared for the emotional price that you may not have expected to pay. Many of us have been under the false illusion that the more successful we become in each domain discussed in this book, the happier others will be for us. The harsh reality that life has continuously taught me is that a vast majority of the time, that belief is, in fact, an illusion.

It is sometimes challenging to realize that while you are committed to utilizing these tips to achieve success in multiple areas, everyone else around you may not be. Subsequently, this may mean that everyone around you may not respond to your success in an optimistic or affirming way. My individual journey has taught me that there will be a range of responses to your success. Everyone's expression regarding your success will not be what you had expected or hoped for. You will indeed have to learn to manage your emotional reactions to the responses of others.

In some instances, people will respond in a supportive and loving way. They will embrace the fact you have achieved success that many have never even dreamed of aspiring to reach. The fact that you may be one of the only people in your family to have set out on such a unique journey and to have accomplished it is worthy of the compliments you will receive.

This is just what you may have expected and what you have been giving others as they have accomplished their goals, only to set their course for an even bigger goal. In other instances, however, you will have those who will look at your success as a personal report card for their achievements.

While you were expecting them to be happy for you, they are happy inside yet outside, they are exhibiting shock and surprise that your goals were even attainable. This reflection may cause them to feel as though they are less successful or not as accomplished as they thought they were.

People often use others to measure their level of success, and you have just redefined success in their eyes, which can be a bit much to take in at one time. This feeling of inadequacy or sense of failure has nothing to do with you. Yet, it will come across as though they are not genuinely happy for you and your success. They may be thinking to themselves that if they had known it was that easy, they would have done it, too. They may not understand it really was not easy. You just chose not to complain all along the way, nor did you find it important to tell everyone how many times you had failed or had minor setbacks when they asked you, "So how are things going?"

You see, everyone shares their tests once they have become testimonies as to how they overcame them. The challenge with that is while you are going through your cocoon phase and making the needed changes to accomplish your goals, someone else is not in a cocoon and so once you become a butterfly, they will be wondering why they have not.

Do not internalize their reflection as not being happy for you. Know that everyone has their own journey and each one starts by taking the first step. The first step is the hardest one. You have taken the first step, and I applaud you for reading this book and for taking the actions necessary to reach your goals.

You are already a winner. Now it is time to act on what you have learned to prove it to yourself and to claim your rewards. Congratulations on your success and I wish you the best of luck as you continue to set and achieve new goals for yourself. Remember, you're closer than you think!

Contact Teeba about:

Speaking Engagements

Teeba Rose is known for his infectiously enthusiastic and energetic presentations that keep his audiences at the edge of their seats wanting more. As a successful entrepreneur, author and speaker, Teeba uses his thought-provoking presentations to move his audiences to the next level. His unique perspective and delivery makes Teeba Rose a sought-after and one-of-a-kind speaker.

To have Teeba Rose speak at your next conference, commencement or company event, please contact:

Website: www.teebarose.com

Email: teeba@teebarose.com

P.O Box 31776
Houston, Tx 77231

Sharing your story

I want to hear your story on how this book has helped you or someone you know. As I travel the country and share this information with people, I love to hear about the impact that it has had in their lives. I would love to hear your story. Please send it to me at teeba@teebarose.com.

Teeba Rose

ABOUT THE AUTHOR

As a speaker, real estate investor and entrepreneur, Teeba Rose believes we all desire to live a good life; we just take different paths to get there. A native Houstonian, Teeba holds a bachelor's degree in marketing and a master's in community development and has held positions with Xerox and Abbott Laboratories, both fortune 500 companies. Whether he's addressing a crowd of over 15,000 people, or mentoring hardworking college students, Teeba always gives 110%. His wife and two wonderful children are his motivation every day.

Teeba Rose

YOU'RE CLOSER
Than you Think:

THE WORKBOOK

YOUR PLAN FOR SUCCESS

A wise man once said, "You do not have to be great to start, but you do have to start to become great."". To that end, I believe this workbook is a practical guide that will help you assess where you are and determine what you need to modify and adjust to move you closer to the life you desire.

Table of Contents

Vision Board Exercise

The first action step that you need to do in order to move closer to the life you desire is to create a vision board. Millions of people create vision boards. A vision board is much like today's Pinterest. It is a collage of things you would like to accomplish placed on a board about 24 x 36 inches in size. This board should reflect in pictures, symbols or words your goals. You can get the aforementioned specifics from magazines or the Internet. Purchase card stock or a large board (perhaps from Hobby Lobby or Lowes) and get started with posting pictures, symbols and words from magazines or the Internet that reflect your goals for the next year.

You may ask why this step is so important. Well, studies have shown that there is a direct correlation between visually seeing your goals and achieving them. When your goals are in view on your vision board, they will be at the forefront of your mind thus motivating you to accomplish them.

Time Maximization Exercise (pg. 1– 6)

One way to ensure that you are on the right path to achieving your goals is to ensure that you are maximizing your time. The time maximization exercise will give you greater insight into how you are spending your time with the hope of better maximizing it.   This exercise should be done in three steps: First, for the upcoming week, write down the events within your day. Second, calculate the time you spent each day engaging in each activity. Third, reflect on how you have spent your time and identify areas in which you can improve.

Part 1: Describe your Daily Activities

Monday

5:00am_____

6:00am_____

7:00am_____

8:00am_____

9:00am_____

Teeba Rose

10:00am_____

11:00am_____

12:00pm_____

1:00pm_____

2:00pm_____

3:00pm_____

4:00pm_____

5:00pm_____

6:00pm_____

7:00pm_____

8:00pm_____

9:00pm_____

10:00pm_____

11:00pm_____

12:00am_____

Tuesday

5:00am_____

6:00am_____

7:00am_____

8:00am_____

9:00am_____

10:00am_____

11:00am_____

12:00pm_____

1:00pm_____

2:00pm_____

3:00pm_____

4:00pm_____

5:00pm_____

6:00pm_____

7:00pm_____

8:00pm_____

9:00pm_____

10:00pm_____

11:00pm_____

12:00am_____

Wednesday

5:00am_____

6:00am_____

7:00am_____

8:00am_____

9:00am_____

10:00am_____

11:00am_____

12:00pm_____

You're Closer Than You Think

1:00pm_____

2:00pm_____

3:00pm_____

4:00pm_____

5:00pm_____

6:00pm_____

7:00pm_____

8:00pm_____

9:00pm_____

10:00pm_____

11:00pm_____

12:00am_____

Part 2: Calculate the time spent on daily activities

Monday

How much time did you spend:

Preparing to leave for work_____

Getting to and from work_____

Working _____

Working on personal self-development_____

Exercising_____

Watching TV_____

Working on short-term goals_____

Preparing for the next day_____

Relaxing_____

Doing household chores_____

Sleeping_____

Misc._____

Tuesday

How much time did you spend:

Preparing to leave for work _____

Getting to and from work_____

Working _____

Working on personal self- development_____

Exercising_____

Watching TV_____   _____

Working on short-term goals_____

Preparing for the next day_____

Relaxing_____

Doing household
chores_____

Sleeping_____

Misc. _____

Wednesday

How much time did you spend:

Preparing to leave for work_____

Getting to and from work_____

Working _____

Working on personal self- development_____

Exercising_____

Watching TV_____

Working on short-term goals

_____

Preparing for the next day_____

Relaxing_____

Doing household chores_____

Sleeping_____

Misc._____

Thursday

How much time did you spend:

Preparing to leave for work _____

Getting to and from work_____

Working _____

Working on personal self- development_____

Exercising_____

Watching TV_____

Working on short-term goals

_____

Preparing for the next day_____

Relaxing_____

Doing household chores_____

Sleeping_____

Misc._____

Friday

How much time did you spend:

Preparing to leave for work_____

Getting to and from work_____

Working _____

Working on personal self- development_____

Exercising_____

Watching TV_____

Working on short-term

goals_____

Preparing for the next day_____

Relaxing_____

Doing household chores_____

Sleeping_____

Misc._____

Now that you can see how much time you exerted daily engaging in each activity, consider the following questions:

What didn't you get done that you could have?_____

Why didn't it get done?_____

What should you do less of ?_____

What can you do more of?_____

How many more hours can you devote to your goal?_____

With this restructuring of time, what will you do differently?_____

How much time will you set aside to prepare for the next day?_____

What time on Sunday will you plan out your upcoming week?_____

Part 3 :Making Improvements

Maximizing your time will not happen overnight. It will involve a critical evaluation of how you spend your time followed by the implementation of better habits where necessary. Using the data you have above, identify the areas in which your time is not maximized. Next, start today employing the tips listed below to help you better maximize your time.

Time Maximization Tips

- Create an overview of what you would like to accomplish each week on Sunday.
- Utilizing a planner (paper or electronic), create a to-do list for each day.
- Go over tomorrow's plan the night before.
- Review your day at the end of the day and make modifications for tomorrow.
- To maximize your drive time, you can listen to audio books.

Brand Review and Critique Exercise(pg. 7-16)

Describe what you think your brand is in three words:

_____,_____,_____

In two words, describe what you think your physical

appearance says about

you:_____,_____

Identify three people to interview (e.g., a family member,

friend and co-worker). Inform them that you are

conducting a self-evaluation and ask them to be candid in

their responses. Be prepared to handle their honest

feedback.

Question #1 (**Family Member**): Use three words to describe

me_____,_____,_____

Question #2 (**Family Member**): Use two words to describe

my physical appearance:_____,_____

Question #1 (**Friend**): Use three words to describe

me_____,_____,_____

Question #2 (**Friend**): Use two words to describe my

physical appearance:_____,_____

Question #1 (**Co-worker/Associate**): Use three words to describe

me:_____,_____,_____

Question #2 (**Co-worker/Associate**): Use two words to describe my physical appearance:

_____,_____

What ideally would you like to hear about yourself?_____

Are there any discrepancies in the words that you and others use to describe yourself?

_____

What steps do you need to take to reconcile any discrepancies?

_____

Does your professional attire reflect the position and life that you have or the position and life that you want?

_____

What books are you reading or listening to, to get you closer to your goals?_____

What are you doing for personal self-development?_____

Do the current images of you online match your vision for yourself?_____

Tips for Managing Your Brand

- Be a person of your word. If you say you will, then make sure you do…
- Apply privacy settings to your social media accounts.
- Don't take photos or participate in photos that are not in line with your brand
- Always remember someone has to be successful, so if not you, then who?
- Create a professional profile for yourself on Linked in.
- Have a clear /sharp picture taken of yourself for professional use.

Teeba Rose

Extraordinary Habit Evaluation Exercise (pg.17-26)

Do you put forth 100% in everything you do?_____

What areas do you give 100% effort?_____

_____

_____

_____

What areas do you give less than 100% of your effort?_____

_____

_____

_____

 What percentage of your effort would you say you give to the areas above?_____

_____

_____

_____

How much more energy would it take to give the area

above 100% vs. the percentage

above?_____

_____

Tips for making extraordinary a habit

- Before your day starts, remind yourself that you are going to have a great day.
- Always let your work reflect your brand.
- When you enter a room, be sure to remind yourself that a smile and pleasant greeting are free but go a long way.
- Work as though everyone will see what you produce and one day, they will.
- Let your positive energy be infectious.
- Always give your full effort to what you are working on.
- Let your work ethic be the standard that others follow.
- When you are involved with something, be present and in the moment.
- Walk with purpose and drive. It will remind your body that you are on the move.

- Always arrive 10 – 15 minutes early to scheduled events.
- Choose to maintain a great attitude no matter what comes your way.

Goal Setting Exercise

Identify at least three to four long-term goals (i.e., goals that you would like to accomplish five to10 years from now).

 When identifying goals, ask yourself:

1. What does your best life consist of?_____

2. How is your brand described? What does extraordinary look like for you?_____ _____

3. Are you living within your desired budget?_____

4. How do you give back (time, volunteerism)?_____

5. How much have you saved?_____

6. Have you invested?_____

7. Do you feel successful?_____

Goal 1: _____

Goal 2: _____

Goal 3: _____

Goal 4: _____

Short-Term Goal (12-Month Goal)

Now that you have thought critically about what you would like to accomplish and identified your long-term goals, list three goals that you would you like to accomplish within the next 12 months (i.e., your short-term goals). Your goals must be specific, measurable and attainable. For example: I will earn an additional \$10,000 by December 1st, 2016.

Goal 1: _____

Goal 2: _____

Goal 3: _____

How much time will you commit to accomplishing your goals each week?

Goal 1:_____ hours

Goal 2:_____ hours

Goal 3: _____ hours

Financial Analysis Exercise (pg. 27-46)

Fill in the blanks below to assess your current budget.

Section A

Monthly Expenses

Rent or Mortgage	$
Car Note or Transportation	$
Grocery Bill	$
Eating Out (lunch, dinner, breakfast)	$
Entertainment (parties, drinking, movies, potluck, etc.)	$
Credit Card Bills Minimum Payments	$
Student Loans	$
Other Loans	$
Gas	$
Cable /Netflix	$
Water Bill	$
Utilities	$
Recreation Budget (beauty/ clothing)	$

Pet's Needs	$
Child's School	$
Child's Clothes and Food	$
Car Insurance	$
Health Insurance	$
Incidentals (car repairs, oil change, and other unexpected items)	$
Cell Phone	$
Shopping	$
Home Miscellaneous (yard, pool, light bulbs, repairs)	$
Memberships (gym, etc.)	$
Dry Cleaners	$
Car Wash	$
Savings	$
Investing	$
Giving	$
Miscellaneous	$
Grand Total	$

Section B

Monthly Income

Monthly Income (minus taxes)	$
Part-time Income (minus taxes)	$
Other Businesses	$
Revenue from Investments	$
Grand Total	$

Calculate the dollar amount for each section. Round up to the nearest dollar.

Section A _____ - Section B_____= Section C_____

Section C represents your true net balance and budget at the end of each month. When **Section A** (your expenses) exceeds Section B (your income) you will always have a negative Section C or negative net balance. When Section A and Section B are close to equal, you are officially "living from paycheck to paycheck." Without planning, it does not take much to get to this state. Currently, millions of people are living paycheck to paycheck , and most believe that if they earned more money, they would not be living paycheck to paycheck. That is simply not true. The truth is if you do not change how you spend money, how much money you have will never solve the problem permanently.

Your **needs** will cover your basic necessities such as shelter, clothing, transportation and food.

Your **wants** will convince you to make your needs look better. You know...get a better house/apartment, nicer clothes, more expensive car and fancier foods. Once you have made the decision to get what you want, it is even easier to justify getting the **accessories to your wants.**

List your Assets (anything that you own which brings revenue each month or can be sold for a profit)

Section D

Assets

Savings Account	$
Coins (gold/ silver)	$
Retirement Account	$
Stocks/Bonds	$
% of Ownership in a Business Worth "X"	$
Rental Properties	$
Equity in Your Home	$

Life Insurance	$
Miscellaneous	$
Grand Total	$

Section E

Now List Your Total Liabilities.

Student Debt	$
Credit Card Debt	$
Balance on Your Home	$
Balance on Your Car	$
Personal or Business Loans	$
Total	$

Net Worth

Fill in the results from the section above in the blanks below.

Section D_____ - Section E_____ =

Your Net Worth_____

Your net worth is the value of your financial legacy you would leave behind today. This is your starting point.

In Chapter 4 "Multiply Your Income," you brainstormed several ideas of other sources of income. Now let's put those sources of income in the chart below and the expected income associated with them.

Other Sources of Income

	$
	$
	$
	$
Total	$

Your current income _____+ (the line total from above) _____ = _____your income potential for this year. (If self-employed, remember to subtract 15% from the total number for taxes to determine your take-home amount).

Now that you know your monthly expenses, you can make a few changes to save money to reduce your monthly budget.

When it comes to growing your money, you may need a little help. Fill in the blanks with the business professionals that you would like to use (it is OK if you don't know who they are at this time, but think about this as you meet people)

Real Estate Professional	
Financial Planner	
Insurance Agent	
Banking Professional	

Tips for Managing Your Money

1. Open up different accounts within the same or different institution (credit union or bank). Set your bills up on autopay and have a set amount drafted for savings, investing and giving sent to a separate account.
2. Clip coupons from the local paper.
3. Get your favorite stores' apps to receive electronic coupons delivered right to your phone.
4. Make a list with an estimated total for each item before going to purchase groceries (and stick to the list).
5. Remember to look online for bargains when making a purchase.
6. Buy groceries and prepare your lunch for the week on Saturday or Sunday.

7. Buy clothes and other items in the off season(Jan 1st -Feb 29th and July 4th – Aug 31st) at 75%-85% off.
8. Anywhere that you shop that has a membership club, make sure that you become a member such as Triple A, Walgreens, CVS, Kroger, Sam's and Costco.
9. Consider shopping at thrift shops.
10. Consider purchasing a previously owned automobile to save money.

Credit Evaluation and Solutions Exercise (pg. 47 – 62)

Now that you have assessed your net worth and are aware of how much debt you have, it is important that you know your credit score.

Obtaining your credit report is simple, easy to do, and very convenient. You are given a free credit report each year and obtaining it will not affect your credit score in a negative way to get it. There are several free sites to get your credit report. Here are a few sites for you to use:

www.creditreport.com

www.annualcreditreport.com

www.freescoreonline.com

Look at your report thoroughly and determine if all of the information is true or if there is information that needs to be corrected. If you have information that needs to be corrected, there are several companies that can help you do it. Here are a couple:

www.creditrepair.com

www.consumersadvocate.org

Once you have begun to repair your credit, an optional way to protect it may be to subscribe to a credit monitoring service that will alert you of any negative or derogatory actions and inquiries when it occurs. Below are a couple of credit monitoring services:

www.legalshield.com

www.lifelock.com

To make sure that you are building positive credit, fill in the following:

Credit Card	Limit	Balance	Limit÷Balance = %

Your goal is to get the % down to 30% or below.

Tips for Managing your Credit

- Obtain and review your credit report once or twice a year.
- Get help if needed to clear any disparaging or incorrect information.
- Consider obtaining a credit monitoring service.
- Strive to maintain credit card balances that are 30% or below.

Mentor Selection Exercise (pg. 63-67)

To stay on track, you will need to be around and talk to likeminded people. In the area below, fill in the blanks with whom you would like your mentor(s) to be. The mentors that you choose can be younger or older. Here are a few suggestions when choosing a mentor:

1. The mentor has an area in which he or she is thriving.
2. The mentor is currently employed in a work position that you aspire to be in.
3. The mentor has a relationship that you admire.
4. The mentor exhibits a level of professionalism that you would like to emulate.
5. The mentor has obtained a desirable level of financial success.
6. The mentor is considered a leader.

Mentors

Name   Area of Success

1. _____ / _____

2. _____ / _____

3. _____ / _____

Now that you have a mentor, if you know of other individuals who have similar goals, it would be a great idea to start a mastermind group. This is a group of people that has similar goals. This group can be any age and does not have to be more than two to five people. I would recommend intentionally prioritizing spending time with this group at least once a month. Each person may have a different goal, but the energy and dynamic of pursuing those goals are the same. This group will help you strive towards a greater version of you. Who will be in your mastermind group?

The Mastermind Group

Name **Their Goal**

1. _____ /_____

2. _____ /_____

3. _____ /_____

4. _____ /_____

5. _____ /_____

Teeba Rose

JOURNAL

Please use the following sections as a space to take notes during individual sessions with your mentor(s).

JOURNAL

_____

_____

_____

_____

_____

_____

_____

_____

_____

_____

_____

_____

_____

_____

_____

_____

_____

_____

_____

_____

_____

JOURNAL

_____

_____

_____

_____

_____

_____

_____

_____

_____

_____

_____

_____

_____

_____

_____

_____

_____

_____

_____

_____

_____

_____

JOURNAL

_____

_____

_____

_____

_____

_____

_____

_____

_____

_____

_____

_____

_____

_____

_____

_____

_____

_____

_____

_____

JOURNAL

_____

_____

_____

_____

_____

_____

_____

_____

_____

_____

_____

_____

_____

_____

_____

_____

_____

_____

_____

Teeba Rose

JOURNAL

JOURNAL

_____

_____

_____

_____

_____

_____

_____

_____

_____

_____

_____

_____

_____

_____

_____

_____

_____

_____

_____

_____

_____

JOURNAL

JOURNAL

JOURNAL

_____

_____

_____

_____

_____

_____

_____

_____

_____

_____

_____

_____

_____

_____

_____

_____

_____

_____

_____

JOURNAL

_____

_____

_____

_____

_____

_____

_____

_____

_____

_____

_____

_____

_____

_____

_____

_____

_____

_____

_____

_____

JOURNAL

JOURNAL

_____

_____

_____

_____

_____

_____

_____

_____

_____

_____

_____

_____

_____

_____

_____

_____

_____

_____

_____

Teeba Rose

JOURNAL

JOURNAL

_____

_____

_____

_____

_____

_____

_____

_____

_____

_____

_____

_____

_____

_____

_____

_____

_____

_____

_____

_____

Teeba Rose